EXCLUSION:
who needs it?

by

KAY KINDER
ANNE WILKIN
ALISON WAKEFIELD

Published in March 1997
by the National Foundation for Educational Research,
The Mere, Upton Park, Slough, Berkshire SL1 2DQ

CONTENTS

EXCLUSION: WHO NEEDS IT?

How shall I lose the sin,
yet keep the sense
And love the offender,
yet detest the offence?
Alexander Pope

INTRODUCTION

Recent research, government figures – and the media – report that the numbers of permanent exclusions are rising in both the primary and secondary school sectors. Data from LEAs which have been explored by researchers such as Hayden (1994), Parsons (1996), Gillborn (1995) and Berridge and Brodie (forthcoming) would also suggest that certain groups are more likely to become excludees – for instance, boys, Afro-Caribbeans, children looked after by the local authority, Year 10-11 pupils, and those with special educational needs.

Beyond the statistics, case-study research and media interest have conveyed just how intensely the exclusion process is experienced by all its protagonists – pupils, parents, governors, teachers, senior school staff, LEA personnel. The intensity of feeling which can surround the process suggests that exclusion is viewed from very different but deeply held value positions. The turbulence which may precede and surround the implementation of an exclusion perhaps signifies a more profound confusion – or at least a lack of consensus – about its very function.

The rise in exclusion rates clearly begs other questions: namely, why is it occurring? What can be done about the increase? And, what effect is the increase likely to have?

Conclusive evidence on these crucial issues of causality and subsequent long-term impact is unlikely to be attained until large-scale and longitudinal research is commissioned. At the moment, on these issues there seems to be only more or less informed opinion from a wide range of protagonists. Yet if viewpoints on the purpose of exclusion vary, no doubt the key questions of cause, effect and solution will also elicit different responses. Such variance, in turn, might be seriously reducing the possibility of consensus, consistency and cooperation in any subsequent involvement in the exclusion process.

For this reason, this report attempts to contribute to the debate on exclusion by offering an overview of a range of perspectives on the issue. It is based on interview data collected from school and LEA staff, parents and pupils.

BACKGROUND

The third phase of a wide-ranging research project (funded by the NFER Membership Programme), entitled 'School Attendance, Truancy and Exclusions' sought to collect the views of a sub-sample of mainstream practitioners who had been involved in the exclusion process and LEA or behavioural support staff who had subsequent involvement with excludees.

This sub-sample, drawn from 15 schools and six off-site units in 15 LEAs, comprised 41 school staff and 25 LEA staff or those working in off-site provision within LEA-based services.

The questions on exclusion formed a discrete section of the interview schedule and covered:

- perceptions of the value and purpose of exclusion;
- views on why the number of permanent exclusions was increasing;
- whether schools could do more to limit exclusions; and
- opinions on what should happen to permanent excludees.

Put together, this practitioner sample is clearly not, nor was intended to be, representative. However, it does offer a range of perspectives which are perhaps closest to the actual experience and outcomes of exclusion, rather than from those who are mainly familiar with an exclusion's formal procedures (e.g. governors) or the pupil behaviours or incidents implicated in or preceding exclusion (e.g. class teachers or form tutors).

THE PURPOSE OF EXCLUSION

The question concerning the purpose and value of an exclusion was discussed with interviewees, and the tenor of their answers, whilst often recognising the complexity and overlap of the issues, fell into three main categories:

- exclusion as the action of **removal**
- exclusion as the act of **reprisal**
- exclusion as the avenue for **remedy**.

Exclusion as the action of removal

From this viewpoint, an exclusion's function was to remove those behaviours which caused unacceptable disruption to the learning and/or social processes of the school. Thus, its primary beneficiary was seen to be those pupils and staff who had experienced some degree of disturbance, distress or possible danger as a result of proximity to the excluded pupil.

In order to explain the exclusion in these removal terms, a utilitarian rationale was applied: namely that any interests or advantages which the excluded pupil may have in remaining at (or returning to) the school were outweighed by the needs and rights of the rest. The school could not – or should not – meet the needs of the excluded pupil, and its resources and skills were insufficient to handle those needs – or indeed, in principle, should not be diverted in that direction. Exclusion was essentially a means of protecting the learning and social environment of the school community.

This viewpoint was sometimes accompanied by applying descriptors to an excluded pupil type (such as 'thug', 'unteachable' or 'young criminal') which further pinpointed their non-acceptability as a 'mainstream pupil'. However, this type of language might result in the notion of non-acceptable behaviour eliding into a judgement of disruptive pupils as being less deserving, and indeed 'exclusion as removal' clearly could be interpreted and experienced as discriminatory, rejecting or 'failing' the excluded child. Beyond that, it was sometimes implied that the 'exclusion as removal' rationale became a way of manipulating or deselecting a school's clientele, as pupils with behavioural difficulties were a tax on the reputation, and academic achievement, of a school.

	Exclusion as ...
... removal	LEA officer: *Some exclusions seem to be about PR for the school; some heads liked to be seen to be taking a firm line on discipline and this led to a rise in exclusions. Certain heads have used exclusion as a way of improving their schools – they introduce a very strict discipline code and that results in quite considerable numbers of exclusions – but then that high level of exclusion shows no sign of abating – it's giving the school a reputation as a school that doesn't take any nonsense and that appeals to parents in some instances. But, it puts a strain on LEA resources. At one stage, one head was excluding pupils for non-attendance – it was clear he had an eye on certain types of performance indicators.* BSS coordinator: [In some schools] *there's a belief that by purely telling pupils to behave they will behave; their view is 'We do not namby-pamby our children here. We don't need to be hugely supportive because the ethos we run here is that everyone will behave, and if we give support we are implying everyone doesn't have to behave, because we are going to be supportive'. These schools see the answer lies only with the child, who must choose to behave, and if they don't, they won't remain in the school. There's no notion that children might need support in managing their behaviour.* Head: *I feel that the whole system of exclusions has got completely out of hand. We tend to rely on exclusions 'cos it's the easiest thing to do, to get rid of them. I think we are disenfranchising a whole generation, putting them on the streets, and you're just saying to them 'You're a failure, you've lost all round'.* Head: *Because it's easy, it's far easier to actually just exclude them, 'cos as far as the school's concerned, it gets them out of school, it gets them out of that staff's hair. The member of staff thinks 'Yes, I've been supported'. But is it really going to have any material effect on that child, and if it hasn't what's its purpose?*

Key questions might be:

- Does 'exclusion as removal' limit the need for or ability of schools to reflect on their own systems and procedures for dealing with behavioural difficulties or to examine those factors within the school which may contribute to disruptive behaviour ?

- Does accepting the 'exclusion as removal' argument fail to recognise and applaud those schools and staff who work hard to retain pupils experiencing behavioural problems?

Exclusion as the act of reprisal

Exclusion, when viewed as the act of reprisal, performed the function of being the supreme sanction by which a school indicated its non-acceptance of certain pupil behaviours. The purpose was essentially defined as a punishment, and centred on being the deserved consequence of nonconformity to school expectations. That punishment's purpose was sometimes described by practitioners as largely symbolic – a deterrent to others, even an act of revenge or retribution – or as a way of inculcating contrition (and hence 'solving' the bad behaviour) by setting in motion deprivation of such things as social opportunities, home privileges or loss of adult approval – which the young person would not want to recur.

Respondents offering this perception often reflected on the limitation of exclusion as a reprisal, or rather suggested that its effectiveness related to assumptions of contrition-consequence which all too rarely appertained to those excluded – at least at the point of exclusion. The key to success often lay in parental involvement with the reprisal and in many instances this reinforcement was not possible.

'Fitness for purpose' became a key issue in this use of exclusion. School staff referred to lack of other options within their sanction repertoire which resulted in the use of exclusion even though the likelihood of it resolving or curing difficult behaviour was doubtful.

	Exclusion as ...
... reprisal	Deputy head: *I find teachers are very simplistic about the 'something needs to be done' issue. I don't think people have any great rationale about why they want exclusions, particularly fixed term exclusions. How does three days' exclusion change a situation, is it successful? It's just part of the 'something needs to be done' notion, and it is done ... it's retributive, and I would argue very strongly that retribution is a very small part of what we are about in educational establishments.* Head: *Support for staff isn't always best shown by removing a child from the school – because there will soon be another child that will just replace that one. We have got to bear some responsibility for the behaviour of our children – and I think we have a duty to children [in] a school like ours, where there are a large number of children coming from dysfunctional families, because if all you can do is threaten to throw them out and then ultimately put them out, what happens to a community when you've got a large number that would apply to?* Senior teacher: *Sometimes we use the exclusion not for that child but to actually show others that we mean business, others that might be on the fringe of problems ... it's to send messages to a variety of people. We must show kids that their behaviour can't go on – we've got to set the tone for the school. There aren't many options and they are hard to resource – internal exclusions is a heavy workload and monitoring and counselling is so time-consuming.* Deputy head: *What we are disciplining is the overt challenge to the system in this building ... and in that sense my answer is the exclusion might not do much for the child, but we've so few sanctions that we have to send that signal that this is unacceptable. And you've got to think of the majority of the kids and creating a learning environment in which they can succeed, and sometimes the exclusion might be symbolic, and it might be a whitewash job, but you're taking a disruptive kid out of the system, you're forcing a situation of parental interview but you're really sending a signal to the other kids 'Look this ain't on'.*

Key questions might be:

- What are the ramifications of operating a reprisal that is perceived to be neither an effective nor appropriate 'punishment' for many individual pupils?

- How far can exclusions operate as an effective deterrent for other pupils?

- What other strategies might be employed so that staff can feel supported in the light of non-acceptable and difficult behaviour by pupils?

Exclusion as the avenue for remedy

In this function, exclusion was seen primarily as serving the best interest of the pupil, implying a recognition that, either temporarily or permanently, the young person would gain most benefit from alternative or additional educational provision. The context or content of that provision needed to be changed: pupils were failing to cope within a mainstream setting and required additional support in terms of greater individual attention, smaller group settings, therapeutic intervention or an alternative type of learning experience – vocational, work placements, etc.

Exclusion was then a way of signalling or instigating action to support the pupil experiencing behavioural difficulties.

	Exclusion as ...
... remedy	BSS coordinator: *A lot of children fall out of school, things start to go wrong, they build up a great crescendo, and children become very entrenched and can't get out of the difficulties they are in and are actually not going to succeed in the school they're in, they need space.*
	Head of PRU: *For some who can't cope and to actually go to a PRU, with the aim to come back to mainstream, gradually be fed into the system again – but there needs to be work BEFORE he's back in mainstream - every time he's excluded he's getting more and more negative, and more disaffected, and he thinks 'Why should I try, they don't want me, no school wants me'.*
	BSS teacher: *I don't think schools are necessarily ideal places for all pupils – school is a certain institution, some aren't suited to it, some are – but we punish those who aren't suited.*
	Head: *Some pupils clearly need provision other than mainstream school; sometimes the only way their needs are going to be noted or looked at is if they go to an extreme situation where they are excluded.*

Key questions:

- Is 'exclusion as remedy' – with its implication of meeting need – always best delivered via a procedure which carries other connotations of very public and overtly punitive rejection?

- Does 'exclusion as remedy' currently allow sufficient opportunities for recovery and reintegration?

THE RISE IN EXCLUSION: CAUSES AND SOLUTIONS

The sample of mainstream practitioners and specialist LEA support staff were asked to comment on what, in their view, might be causing the increase in exclusions and then what they felt could be done, at school level, to limit this escalation. Any differences in the two sub-samples' responses were noted, as lack of consensus on causes and solutions might illustrate yet again how the exclusion issue can come to reverberate with tension due to distinct or disparate viewpoints.

Four major arenas were cited as key reasons underpinning the rise in exclusions:

- **general pupil disaffection factors**
  e.g. lack of curriculum relevance, home and social background, lack of respect for authority

- **the current educational climate and policy**
  e.g. league tables, school marketing

- **the exclusion process itself**
  e.g. lack of consistency between schools, the lack of other sanctions

- **lack of resources and training**
  e.g. the need for more support/expertise in learning and behavioural problems.

There was much consensus among all the respondents about these factors, particularly in the arena of resources and training. Recurring issues here included the lack of sufficient external support for learning and behavioural needs, particularly in the area of the Code of Practice on the Identification and Assessment of Special Educational Needs; lack of specialist staff, time and expertise within mainstream schools for dealing with behavioural difficulties; and a need for initial teacher training (ITT), NQT induction and INSET to focus more on the management of behaviour.

Beyond the resource issue, it was notable that school staff were rather more likely to pinpoint general disaffection factors, expressing the perceived tensions inherent in delivering a curriculum of sometimes questionable relevance to an increasingly disengaged and dysfunctional pupil clientele. LEA staff often concurred with this view, but also gave more prominence to the current educational climate and the exclusion process itself, which allowed some schools to exclude too readily pupils who were in fact 'redeemable' or manageable. Thus, a slight variation in emphasising either the pathology of excludees or the procedures of exclusion as a major cause in increase was evident. This might perhaps signal a possible source of tension between these key players in the exclusion process.

That being the case, the issue of what schools might be able to do to restrict the numbers of exclusions was an important area of inquiry. In the recent OFSTED (1996) report on secondary school exclusions, five factors were identified as *'crucial in influencing a school's success in reducing exclusion'* (para. 43, p. 16). These were: *'effectiveness of the school behaviour policy; the application of suitable rewards and sanctions, the effectiveness of strategies to monitor exclusion, the quality of pastoral support and the extent of curriculum modification'*. Staff training, parental involvement and SEN provision were also mentioned. These issues were also touched on by our practitioner sample.

However, given that the key factors accounting for a rise in excluded pupils identified above often pinpointed some deficit of resources or expertise within the school, it is not surprising that the sample expanded on this when asked about remedies and action to limit exclusions.

Thus, strongly recommended were more resources, in terms of staff and time, for school and LEA specialists to intervene at an earlier stage in any learning and behavioural difficulties; more focus on preventative work in primary schools; more behaviour management training for practitioners and more vocational curriculum opportunities for the disaffected pupil.

Other factors raised which were attainable within existing school resources, included the need for consistent behaviour policies which were devised, adopted and frequently reviewed by the whole school, including pupils and parents; the ongoing involvement with parents; a sanction system which had many small steps prior to exclusion; and a school ethos that put emphasis on reward systems and praise.

Beyond that, some specific actions were suggested which involved attitudinal changes by the excluding school or pro-exclusion lobby, rather than funding or organisational implications. These actions hinged on reappraising behavioural difficulties as a valid special learning need. Further suggestions were that schools might also reflect on their own contribution to disaffection – in terms of the quality of the interpersonal relationships and learning opportunities which they offered pupils. Greater analysis by schools of any patterns in their behavioural problems – both general trends within the school and individual pupils' behavioural cycles – was another issue raised.

Put together, these attitudinal factors were clearly reflecting a value position which suggested that a primary function and ethos of the school was to recognise, diagnose and meet pupils' individual needs, including behavioural difficulties. Rather than creating a culture of implacable conformity, it was the philosophy of inclusion which should drive school policies and strategies associated with behaviour management – including reintegration.

WHAT SHOULD HAPPEN TO PERMANENT EXCLUDEES?

The sample were asked their opinion on the most appropriate next stage for permanent excludees. Whilst acknowledging that a very few severely damaged pupils did require specialist placements, respondents showed considerable accord in their view that, for most youngsters, early reintegration back into mainstream education was the most desirable step after exclusion. School was the place for a young person to find the most valuable type of socialisation and educational opportunity.

In this way, off-site provision would have to be seen as a temporary stage within the process of remedy. Its function would include providing a cooling-off period, offering assessment of need, intensive work on self-esteem, taking responsibility, learning the role of pupil and, very importantly, focusing on curriculum achievement. Thus, attendance at a PRU was not merely a punishment, part of 'exclusion as reprisal'; nor was it a 'sin-bin' for permanently containing (and in effect marginalising) those who were deemed to require removal from mainstream at some point in their school career.

However, reintegration required **planning, resources, focused support** and **correct timing**: without these, any attempt to re-enter mainstream education was often doomed to become simply a reinforcement of failure.

Off-site providers spoke consistently of:

- the need for an assurance of an alternative school place at the point of exclusion;

- a period of six to eight weeks at a PRU being the optimum length of stay, or at least a flexible action plan that could capitalise on the period when a pupil showed a readiness to return to mainstream;

- a programme of reintegration giving individualised support to the youngster on re-entry, which included involvement of the receiving school (such as pre-entry visits, classroom and pastoral support); and

- the benefit of exclusion activating the involvement of other agencies – social services or health.

Looking at these kinds of reintegration goals and strategies, exclusion can indeed be seen as a remedy and, that being so, begins to beg the question again: is it always necessary to go through the exclusion process in order for the youngster to receive such specialised support and therapeutic intervention? Perhaps not surprisingly, pre-exclusion support packages, dual registration at PRUs and school, nurturing classes, within-school units, etc. were seen as a part of the ways forward for LEA Support Services and mainstream schools to collaborate in limiting the emotional and social damage which exclusion operated as merely 'removal' or 'reprisal' might bring in its wake.

*Progress is impossible without change; and
those who cannot change their minds
cannot change anything.*
G. B. Shaw

BACKGROUND

This section of the report reviews the topic of exclusion using the viewpoints and experiences of pupils. It attempts to look at the important issue of how – or whether – exclusion works from a pupil perspective and, in addition, tries to address how far the purposes 'removal', 'reprisal' and 'remedy' might suffuse pupil thinking. The question of what exclusion actually achieves or represents for pupils may well need to be clarified, if the debate about the efficacy of exclusion – at national, LEA and school level – is to progress.

To this end, there was a further data analysis using the responses of 130 secondary-age pupils who had discussed exclusion with researchers during the interview programme of the NFER project on disaffection which took place between the summer term of 1995 and the summer term of 1996. A standard pupil interview included questions covering:

- personal experience of fixed-term and/or permanent exclusion (including reasons for the exclusion);

- how excludees felt about being excluded; and

- any impact or difference the exclusion had made.

Pupils who said they had never been excluded were invited to discuss these issues using their knowledge of other youngsters who had, and many could readily refer to the experiences and attitudes of their peers, friends or siblings.

In all, the views of 28 pupils in off-site provision and 102 from mainstream schools were collected. The majority of these comments therefore referred to fixed-term exclusion and were analysed in several ways:

(i)   A quantitative overview and ranking of the range of reactions to and effects of exclusion.

(ii)   A comparative analysis of any notable variation in responses. (It was felt that a useful categorisation of the data would be to examine differences between three distinct 'exclusion perspectives', namely, those from the non-excludees (47 in total); those of fixed-term excludees (64) and finally the sub-sample of 19 youngsters who had experience of permanent exclusion.)

(iii)   A qualitative analysis of some of the personal 'stories' behind an exclusion and its impact on the youngster. (To this end, a small number of the pupil sample engaged in a case-study/ethnographic-type investigation, involving a series of informal discussions with a researcher to elicit fuller accounts of attitudes and personal biographies.)

PUPIL PERCEPTIONS OF EXCLUSION – AN OVERVIEW

The interview questions encouraged pupils to consider their reactions and feelings at the point of an exclusion as well as its subsequent impact. The sample conveyed a wide range of responses and many of their views replicated practitioners' thinking, as outlined in the previous chapter.

Of course, each story behind an exclusion – whether permanent or fixed-term – was different, and often revealed a unique compound of conflicting responses: the youngster might be both angry yet remorseful, s/he might express indifference to the sanction but also feel sadly isolated from their social world. Notwithstanding this, it was possible to see two distinct trends in the pupil accounts. Exclusion was either generally **accepted** or **resisted** as a reprisal. Thus, initial reactions to the sanction might be expressed in terms of fear and distress, while at the other end of the continuum some pupils would suggest their immediate response to an exclusion was that it was merely 'fun' or a pleasing escape. In the longer term, accepting the exclusion as reprisal would be associated with statements of contrition and regret, while those resisting the sanction would refer to feelings of antagonism to the school, victimhood, indifference and so on. This can be represented diagrammatically as follows:

	ACCEPTANCE of exclusion	RESISTANCE of exclusion
IMMEDIATE RESPONSE **Exclusion is experienced as** ...	distress/ emotional discomfort	escape/fun
LONGER-TERM OUTCOME **Exclusion results in** ...	contrition/regret	antagonism/ indifference

Acceptance of exclusion

Those pupils who indicated that exclusion was, in effect, **accepted** as a serious sanction, often referred to a number of different initial feelings of emotional discomfort, e.g. disappointment, distress, fear or shock at being in so much trouble. Particularly noticeable within these accounts of discomfort was some pupils' fearful anticipation of their parents' reaction to the exclusion, which they recognised would enhance the severity of the reprimand.

Acceptance of exclusion is experienced as ...	
... distress	Permanent excludee: *I was disappointed because I'd ruined everything, like from going from a good school ... even though I knew I wasn't going to learn, it was still disappointing because of the reputation of the school and I was just proud to be in there.*
	Fixed-term excludee: *I felt sorry for myself and wished I hadn't done it.*
	Fixed-term excludee: *I felt bad, like I was naughty and that.*
	Fixed-term excludee: *Shocked, really. I wasn't shocked as in 'been in a crash', shocked ... shaken up ... I was just ... I can't put a word to it ... I couldn't believe it.*
	Permanent excludee: *I was shocked, I didn't know what I'd done until the teacher says 'Well you've done this and you're not doing that and we've had enough', and so they just threw me out. I didn't think it was fair at the time but when the letter came and there was all that and I goes 'Oh I remember that, oh yes I did misbehave in that lesson'.*
	Fixed-term excludee: [I felt] *frightened 'cos my mum and dad weren't there.*
... concern about parental reaction	Fixed-term excludee: ... [I felt] *upset, like worried, 'cos I thought my mum were going to kill me after what I did ...*
	Fixed-term excludee: ... [I felt] *gutted, 'cos I knew I'd get wronged at home.*
	Fixed-term excludee: *I just felt dead sad and that I was letting my mum and dad down ... I've got four sisters and one brother and they were saying 'They've never done anything like this before', and felt like I wasn't one of the family ... mum and dad were really upset ...*

In the longer term, acceptance of exclusion as reprisal was often described in association with some sense of loss (e.g. of social opportunities at school; home privileges; a threat to academic achievement) or simply lack of stimulus/boredom. This list begins to confirm some of the characteristics of pupils for whom the exclusion itself might be a straightforward corrective already identified by practitioners: namely, those youngsters who were socially and/or academically motivated, and those whose parents carried authority and supported school values. By inference, disadvantage or dysfunctionality in inter-personal relations, family circumstances or learning achievement were likely to reduce the impact and acceptance of the exclusion.

Acceptance of exclusion results in ...	
... concern about school achievement	Fixed-term excludee: *... I did miss school a lot, I knew my education was falling down, because they said they were going to send some work up, but they never ... so I knew I were dropping behind ...* Permanent excludee: *I know I'd done wrong; at the time you don't think you've done wrong but then ...when you leave the school, you want an education, like something you **want**, you think 'I don't want to be left out and be a dunce when I leave school'.* Fixed-term excludee: *... I didn't like it; I was thinking what work I've missed and stuff so I wouldn't do well in my exams and stuff.*
... parental reinforcement	Non-excludee: *Some people say it's a holiday, and there'll be other people who'll take an attitude like 'Oh I'm not going to do that again', 'cos their parents really gave 'em a hard time.* Fixed-term excludee: *My mum kept me in and I felt horrible.* Fixed-term excludee: *My dad said if I did it again he'd ground me. I don't like being grounded, so I said 'I won't do it again'.*
... deprivation of social opportunities	Non-excludee: *[My friends] wouldn't do it again, I don't think, because even though they had time off school they got very bored, 'cos all their friends were in school, and they were the only ones outside school unless they had older friends.* Permanent excludee *... I was unhappy in a way, because I would miss all my favourite teachers and my friends ...*
... boredom	Fixed-term excludee: *I was bored at home. I was just stuck in the house, I wanted to play on the computer but I'd played on all the games.* Fixed-term excludee: *It was boring 'cos you can do all that at the weekend as well as you'd just had the weekend anyway, and then, like, it's not the holidays so you haven't planned anything ...* Fixed-term excludee: *It was rather boring 'cos I never had no friends to, like, play football with.* Permanent excludee: *I had all that time to do what I liked. But the thing was all my friends were in school and I was out of school, so it got boring after a while.*

Beyond a focus on specific losses, a number of pupils described the outcome of exclusion as instigating a positive change in behaviour and attitude, with, in some cases, ultimately a general regret or an 'unwishing' of that original behaviour. In this sense, exclusion as reprisal had triggered experiences and deprivation which they did not want to recur and hence had emerged as some kind of route to reform and reintegration, although sometimes this 'unwishing' emerged after initial reactions to exclusion had taken the form of resistance.

Acceptance of exclusion results in ...	
... a resolve to improve behaviour	Fixed-term excludee: *I've started behaving more 'cos I don't want to get another one 'cos you get expelled.* Fixed-term excludee: [My behaviour] *changed a lot. I've been working ... trying to work hard as I can for me exams. And I try to respect all the teachers, even me maths teacher.* Non-excludee: *When they come back yes* [they behave better], *but after a few days then they start messing about again. But there was a girl and she got suspended and she came back and she didn't mess about any more.* (Fixed-term excludee: *It has made a difference. I'm not going to cause any trouble with other people any more.*
... unwishing/regret	Permanent excludee: *I realised I went too far, and that I shouldn't have done that. It makes you realise a lot of things that you shouldn't have done, and you look back and say 'Why did I do it?' I was just being stupid; I thought I was being clever.* Permanent excludee: *If I was talking to a pupil I'd say 'Stick to it' sort of thing. 'Don't do what I've done'. I just wish I didn't do it,* [hadn't done] *it.* Permanent excludee: *Well, if I had my choice, I wish I'd never even* **got** *excluded at all, 'cos it's hard for me even to get another job ... it's really hard and I'm regretting it now – 'cos when you get branded as excluded, you automatically get thought of as bad, but there are lots of different reasons for being excluded.* Permanent excludee: *You think it's hard at first, you know, 'I've been excluded', but it gets boring and you start thinking about it, about your education and what you'll do when you leave school. Being excluded did help me change. They think it's hard at first until you've been out for ages and then it gets horrible.*

Notwithstanding these acceptance statements, a key question must be whether exclusion as a route for reform is effective – or cost-effective – in many instances. For this reason, the views of those pupils who revealed somewhat less contrition in their accounts need also to be considered.

Resistance to exclusion

It was certainly the case that exclusion was **resisted** as a reprisal/reform route by certain pupils, given that initial reactions were expressed as predominantly those of relief/escape or fun. Rather than feeling (or at least admitting) the deprivations and discomfort of an exclusion, being excluded was expressed as a pleasing extrication. Indeed, it might be said that, instead of instigating any reform, these pupils chose to articulate their experience of exclusion as reinforcing existing attitudes and behaviour.

Resistance to exclusion is experienced as ...	
... fun	Non-excludee: *Most people, they see it as fun to be suspended, because when you're suspended for three days it's not like you're bunking off; the school actually **told** you to stay away from school for a couple of days, so they don't see anything bad about it 'cos you get a three-day holiday to do what you want. It's like they're doing you a favour really.*
	Non-excludee: [My mate enjoyed being off], *'cos he could do what he wanted to, like he didn't get grounded or nothing.*
	Non-excludee: *They reckon it's ace ... not coming to school.*
	Fixed-term excludee: *They all, like, laugh at you and stuff if you've been sent home; they think at least you've got out of your lesson and that, but, like, they're all the people who don't do well in this school and stuff, who think it's a holiday and stuff ...*
	Permanent excludee: *I thought 'Yeah' – it was great ... didn't have to get up early in the morning, did no homework, like, just free time.*
	Fixed-term excludee: *When they suspended me, that was exactly what I wanted them to do, and they did it; they did it three times. I wanted time off school and they did it – I were loving every minute of it. I thought 'What are they doing? This is stupid'.*
... a relief	Permanent excludee: *... I was also kind of relieved because I thought 'Now I'm out of there I might be able to get a new beginning ...' ... the second school, when I was expelled I didn't really care, I was just glad to get out of there.*
	Permanent excludee: *I was relieved to just get out; I felt glad because I didn't like that school at all. So it was like a break for me.*
	Permanent excludee: *I used to love it* [being excluded]. *I used to love not going to school. Honestly and truly I hated school ... well high school anyway.*

Other resistance statements suggested that pupils could experience a strong sense of being let down and rejected, or of suffering an injustice. It was the school that in some way was failing them. Such reactions might well have particular associations with exclusion as removal, in that the institution's decision was not felt to be related to the individual pupil's needs or interests, but was experienced as a dismissal of them.

Resistance to exclusion is experienced as ...	
... a sense of injustice	Fixed-term excludee: [I felt] *mad, 'cos even though I had a fight I thought I shouldn't have got suspended.* Fixed-term excludee: *It's just like all the teachers listen to each other and they're right; their version's right and whatever anyone else has to say ...*
... feeling let down/ rejected	Permanent excludee: *I'd been excluded, I'd been excluded again, I'd been excluded again ... it's just a day in the life of* [me]. *They say 'You're excluded, bye' and you say 'Fair enough, bye, see you next week when you'll tell me again'.* Permanent excludee: *I felt let down, I felt that I'd really let down my mum and myself. I mean it wasn't a major thing I'd done...It was just all those little things that built up and built up and after a while the school had had enough. I couldn't really complain about being kicked out but I felt let down, they didn't want me. 'He's gone, never mind, it's just another pupil.'*

Perhaps not surprisingly, in the longer term, some pupils described their antagonism to school, their continuing indifference to the sanction, even of acquiring kudos among peers. Thus, the corollary of exclusion was the rejection or 'blocking out' of school norms. Rather than express their sense of being rejected directly, these pupils in some way chose to decry the school or situation that was rejecting them. A small number of pupils felt exclusion had been responsible for – or at least instigated – a decline in their behaviour and academic achievement.

Resistance to exclusion results in ...	
... antagonism	Fixed-term excludee: *... it just made me more angry ... to get even with the teachers.* Permanent excludee: *You feel angry because you get chucked out for something you didn't really do. It should've been the school's problem to sort it all out, but all they did was think they could exclude someone, and it will all go away – but it don't.* [The problem] *just gets bigger.*
... indifference	Non-excludee: *Doesn't make any difference because* [excluded pupils] *don't really care.* Fixed-term excludee: *I wasn't bothered.* Fixed-term excludee: *I didn't feel too bad really 'cos I could have done what I liked ...*
... kudos/bravado	Non-Excludee: *... the lads and that, they think 'cos they've been suspended it's good and they'll carry it on 'cos they'll think they're Mr Big and 'I'm hard 'cos I've been suspended', and they get expelled and they think they're even more better, and then they've got to go to another school.* Non-excludee: *... most people show off and say 'Oh look, I've been suspended'.*
... adverse effects on work	Fixed-term excludee: *When I did get suspended, that's when everything went downhill because I had to catch up on all me work – a week's worth of work. I've still never caught up with that. That's when all my work went downhill.* Fixed-term excludee: *It just made us worse in school.* Fixed-term excludee: *... with them doing that* [i.e. excluding me], *I missed out on all the work and I didn't want to come to school. Then I were given work, and I didn't want to do that because I wanted to carry on with the work I was doing, 'cos I didn't want to feel left behind.*

Put together, this wide range of responses suggests there are a number of possible routes to reintegration which might occur after the sanction of exclusion and equally might demonstrate why in other instances it manifestly fails to achieve reform.

A rank ordering of these exclusion response types for the sample as a whole was as follows:

RESISTANCE	ACCEPTANCE
• extrication: feeling of escape/relief/ fun	
	• resolve to improve behaviour
	• feeling of distress/emotional discomfort
	• sanction severity reinforced by parents
	• displeasure at missing school (social)
• feeling of injustice/antagonism to school	
• nil-impact/no change	
• indifference	
• kudos	
• adverse effect on work	• concern about parental reaction
• problem of reintegration	
	• impact on return/academic consequences
	• advantageous to other pupils

It is important to stress that this ranking is merely intended to show rough trends and not in any way statistical certainty, and also that the sample comprised mainly disaffected pupils. Nevertheless, it does raise a number of discussion points. First, it should be noted that the most common response, from almost two-fifths (49 respondents) of this sample, suggested an initial reaction to exclusion was in the resistance category 'feeling of escape', compared with less than one in six (19 pupils) referring to immediate emotional discomfort. However, 30 youngsters (nearly a quarter) indicated an outcome of exclusion was the intention to improve behaviour (though, it seemed, not always successfully), while 13 pupils specifically suggested that exclusion had served to ferment or corroborate their sense of victimhood and antagonism to school. Most significantly, reference to parental reaction and subsequent reinforcement of the exclusion as reprisal at home was a feature of some 23 (nearly one in five) pupils' stories of discomfort and unwishing.

PUPIL PERCEPTIONS' OF EXCLUSION: VARIATIONS

While this overview has highlighted variation and contrasts in pupil responses to exclusion, the analysis sought also to identify any notable differences in the viewpoints of the three different types of respondent: non-, fixed-term and permanent excludees. A number of trends were evident.

Most notable in the **non-excludees'** accounts was the fact that more than half cited exclusion as a positive opportunity for extrication, with a particular emphasis on the fun/holiday aspect. Non-excludees' apparent limited awareness of the deprivation of exclusion emerged also in the fact that they rarely mentioned concern about parental reaction or the detrimental implication for their school work; while only one or two indicated the loss of social opportunities at school and the emotional discomfort accompanying exclusion. Perhaps this is significant for the relative impotence of exclusion as a symbolic deterrent/sanction from the pupil perspective: those who had not experienced exclusion in any form were, in essence, pinpointing its non-seriousness. Further, this sub-sample was the most likely to mention how excludees might attempt to gain kudos from an exclusion, suggesting again that certain pupil cultures very publicly resist the sanction's severity. It was non-excludees who stated that exclusion had just 'nil impact' and, not surprisingly, only they suggested that it was other pupils who were advantaged by an exclusion.

Fixed-term excludees' responses were often the stories of extremes. In this group were the youngsters who particularly focused on the sway of parental reaction and reinforcement of the sanction, who expressed concern about their academic record and their displeasure at missing school. Equally, it was the fixed-term excludees who most often described their attempts or intention to improve behaviour immediately following the sanction. In other words, in this group, the privations of exclusion linked most directly to unwishing and regret. They could 'fast-track' to reform. In this way, the possible success of exclusion as some kind of remediating sanction was evident – as long as the pupils showed themselves socially and/or academically motivated, and were backed by authoritative and pro-authority parents. However, resistance statements were evident, with about a third of the fixed-term excludees' accounts suggesting exclusion offered only a pleasing extrication. Significantly, this was a lower response rate than either non- or permanent-excludees. Other comments referred to exclusion as inducing or intensifying antagonism to school, indifference, as well as adverse or nil effects on behaviour and achievement. In these instances, it is possible to conclude that the exclusion may only serve to accelerate the pupil's rejection of school.

The **permanent excludees'** views conveyed a very different and multi-faceted story. Some could relay quite graphically the distress, emotional discomfort and shock they felt at the point of exclusion, which was often intertwined with relief to be extricated from that particular school situation. Indeed, compared with the other sub-samples, permanent excludees' accounts of extrication much more strongly stressed the 'relief/escape' element, implying perhaps some considerable emotional discomfort within the school situation prior to the point of exclusion. They rarely volunteered a concern about parental reaction or reinforcement of the sanction (suggesting perhaps that permanent exclusion was more likely to unite parent and child, or that the youngster was – by this point – beyond parental authority). Overall, with the significant exception of 'missing the social opportunities of school', very few of the permanent excludees' responses were in the categories indicating sanction acceptance. Instead, their perspectives about exclusion contained mostly resistance statements, particularly antagonism to school; a sense of injustice; rejection; and indifference. However, there were strong indications that many of the permanent excludees did reach the point of 'unwishing' their behaviour (and particularly express concern about their education), though – most significantly – rarely as an immediate reaction to permanent exclusion. The implication of this is stark. Successful reintegration is clearly unlikely as long as resistance viewpoints are prevalent in the pupil's thinking, and may explain the difficulty some children have in re-entering mainstream education successfully if they simply carry this array of negative feelings with them. On the other hand, the capacity to change was evident in many instances: behaviour and attitudes were not permanent, even if the title of their penalty was. Following a permanent exclusion, these pupils could eventually reach a point of reform, contrition and desire for reintegration, albeit through a more 'slow-track' procedure.

That being the case, the components of this turn-around needed investigation and here permanent excludees' statements consistently highlighted factors in the off-site provision which they had attended. Almost without exception, the youngsters noted how they were engaging with adults whom they felt gave them respect and regard, as well as clear boundaries of behaviour, and that the learning ambience (especially the low pupil-teacher ratio) was beneficial to their work and motivation. In sum, it suggests an environment where 'what I've done', and 'who I am' are not synonymous. The question raised by this is how far mainstream education can or is willing to replicate these conditions – which clearly do equate with remedy – instead of removing the child in such a disjunctive and terminal way.

Where wrongdoers are confronted within
a continuum of support and respect, then the
process of reintegration can begin.
J. Braithwaite

BACKGROUND

In this short and final section of the report, the views of a sample of parents are conveyed.

During the later stages of the School Attendance, Truancy and Exclusions Project, researchers interviewed a total of 20 parents whose children were being given specific support by their school for attendance and/or behaviour difficulties. These children were part of the project's pupil sample.

Four secondary schools and one primary school from four different LEAs supported this phase of the research. Each school was in an economically deprived area, and in receipt of GEST-funded initiatives which had facilitated strategies to address the needs of disaffected pupils, such as school-based EWOs (educational welfare officers), vocational projects and initiatives to enhance parental involvement.

Access to the parent sample was gained through the support of staff at the school who had actively forged links with home and the community. However, interviews took place in private and usually in the parent's home. The majority of the sample were single parents, and in a number of instances their domestic and/or neighbourhood circumstances involved significant difficulties (including drug-taking, vandalism, crime and sexual abuse).

Although the interview primarily dealt with views about the school strategies which aimed to support their child in mainstream education, each parent was, in addition, asked to give their comments on the issue of exclusion. Eight of the sample were parents whose children had not been excluded (at secondary level, these were mostly pupils exhibiting attendance rather than behavioural difficulties).

The rest had children who had undergone fixed-term exclusion, and two in addition had experienced their child's permanent exclusion.

The views of this distinctive group of parents were important for a number of reasons. They could reflect general parent-consumer opinion which schools and LEAs might encounter. This sample could also provide first-hand accounts of the effects and effectiveness of exclusion as a sanction. They offered a viewpoint – perhaps too rarely heard – from the kinds of social context which might be particularly associated with children's behavioural difficulties in school.

PARENT PERCEPTIONS: AN OVERVIEW

The analysis again looked at how far the purposes of removal, reprisal and remedy characterised the thinking of these parents.

Very noticeably, the idea of exclusion as 'removal' suffused the viewpoints of some parents of non-excludees. Thus, there were comments which suggested that exclusion for miscreant pupils was 'a good idea', '... their due', '... the right thing, if they cause problems and have been given their chances'. One parent clearly articulated the view that excluded pupils were an unnecessary – even undeserving – drain on resources:

> The permanent exclusion of two of my daughters' friends didn't work; they thought it was funny to be off school – but they are now getting home tutors and taking resources away from real needs and problems.

Other parents of non-excludees noted how ineffective they believed exclusion was as a reprisal, indicating that it was 'not strict enough'; '... the system plays into these pupils' hands; they don't see it as punishment'. As the last section has shown, rather like the comments of non-excluded pupils, these opinions suggest very little recognition of the possible discomfort surrounding an exclusion, or the needs and problems that often underpin difficult behaviour. According to this parental view – especially given that an exclusion was thought to have no success in changing behaviour – its primary purpose was to export deviance, and move the problem to a different setting.

Nevertheless, references to insufficient strictness and non-impact do raise an important issue. In effect, these parents may be warning that children cannot actually learn about appropriate behaviour and attitudes when an exclusion is the only consequence of unacceptable conduct.

Indeed, from this same group of non-excludees' parents, there were other comments which pinpointed parental reinforcement as a key factor in the sanction's effectiveness: '*If parents aren't bothered,* [an exclusion] *would have no effect*' and '*Exclusion itself doesn't make much difference; it's the mother coming in to talk to staff that has more effect*'. In other words, exclusion was a reprisal which worked because of action by parents, rather than the school alone.

Some of the parents of fixed-term excludees also stated that it was their corroboration of the reprisal at home which was the crucial component in the effectiveness of an exclusion. Equally, in some comments, parents' continuing support of their child was apparent:

> *I told him how I felt – disappointed – and I explained it. I laid my heart on the line – I told him I hadn't had much schooling. He changed.* [When he was excluded,] *I felt very rough, I was upset, we sat down and talked the punishment over. He didn't like it at all.*

> [When my step-son was excluded,] *he thought he was being clever, but his mum grounded him, and he lost all his treats ... he's not done it since; we supported the school and added our own punishment.*

> *... a day's exclusion for misbehaviour is fun for these kids ... they'd be punished more if made to stay in* [school]. *It didn't match up to the offence. For* [my son], *it was the seriousness of bringing his mum in, not the exclusion which made the difference.*

One parent mentioned their child's boredom during an exclusion as a reason why it was accepted as a reprisal. However, this comment again denotes the support role and authority of the parent in making the sanction work.

> *School should be stricter. R was excluded once – it worked. He suddenly came home with the letter and wouldn't give me it till the morning – he stayed at home and helped me. He learnt; he was bored, he just got bored being away from school.*

In contrast to these views, there were accounts from a number of parents that indicated clearly the nil-impact of a fixed-term exclusion.

> [My son] *would sleep till dinner-time. I gave up and let him sleep and watch telly. He wanted to be suspended; three-day exclusions doesn't help the situation – I'd rather they were in school, and sent to the* [small group withdrawal] *unit.*

> [My child] *has been suspended a few times – a day and now for over a week. He's had to sign a contract, but it's done no good – it doesn't bother him 'cos he doesn't like school. I've kept him in; he hates staying in, but it's not done any good. He doesn't see it as a punishment. He says he'll behave, then he's OK for a couple of days, and then he's back to hisself.*

> *By the stage S was at, suspension wouldn't work –* [kids by then] *feel it's quite good.*

Further explanations for the failure of exclusion to achieve reform were offered by these parents. Often, the inappropriate behaviour by the child was linked to special educational needs, and their personal histories sometimes included early years health problems and/or difficult family circumstances. By and large, the youngster's behaviour was described as involuntary, something which the child could not manage to contain:

> *... it's a mixture of frustration in certain lessons, home and his temper. He isn't very good at reading and writing and when he can't get things down on paper it all builds up and his frustration spills out in bad behaviour.*

> [Exclusion] *doesn't make him behave better; he does things on the spur of the moment and doesn't think about consequences ... he is bored; he's not that clever, he plays up for attention from the other kids, so they'll think he's clever.*

These views on the non-effectiveness of exclusion contrasted sharply with some of the other comments by the parents of fixed-term excludees. On a number of occasions, it was implied that the key component of a child's continuing inclusion in mainstream education was the school's provision of alternative strategies, such as focused pastoral or curriculum support, and especially the forging of positive relations with individual staff members. A full evaluation of the initiatives will feature in a later publication, but extracts from the parent interviews conclude this current section.

These parental-accounts of what lay behind their child's disaffected behaviour and which solutions appeared to be making a difference do suggest that, **rather than reprisals, it is early, sustained and specialised intervention to address behaviour difficulties which may effect some kind of remedy.**

The [vocational] *project allowed S some new authority figures ... [so] the school has done a lot for him. It's been good for his character; he's beginning to respect older people ... from the project, he's now beginning to respect your rules as a mum and as a teacher. It's because he's met no other authority figures except his mum and teachers.*

His EWO [Mrs X] *has been a big influence on him. T is slow – it hurts me to think about it – but now he is thinking for himself, reading, he is trying. X is not his teacher as such; they relate one-to-one. The primary school just went through the motions. Mrs X is the only one to have shown any real interest.*

Since the [vocational] *project, he's calmed, it's calmed him down. It's now making him feel different ... working with other kids in school is good, not sending him out, keeping him with teachers who know him.*

Mr S [in the in-school unit] *is a good influence. He can talk with R – he likes him as a person, gets on with him; if the school has staff that are good with people, they do so much good.*

Parents and teachers can be in two camps. Parents can be afraid to talk to teachers. They see them as teachers, feel like they're going back to school and get patronised by middle-class teachers who don't understand the problems of the estate. [The parental involvement initiative] *did have a definite effect on the kids – they saw parents and teachers as friends and didn't want to offend them that much; they saw us getting on, in a whole new light. Kids see teachers as teachers, not humans with the same feelings ...*

CONCLUSION

This report has tried to offer an analysis of evidence arising from the NFER project 'Truancy, School Attendance and Exclusion', and in so doing has attempted to convey some of the complexity surrounding the topic of exclusion. Undoubtedly, that complexity arises in part because exclusion straddles so many areas where values dominate and often deeply differ. Indeed, exclusion opens up profound issues of debate such as:

- what is appropriate discipline and the purpose of punishment for young people?
- what are the rights and responsibilities of teachers and pupils operating in a school context?
- what are the cures for and causes of young people's behavioural deviance?
- which behavioural difficulties are classifiable as a special need? and
- what are the tensions between the philosophy and practicalities of an inclusive education system?

In pinpointing three major categories or rationales for exclusion – removal, reprisal and remedy – and by identifying reactions of pupils (and parents) to exclusion, the report has revealed some of these conflicting viewpoints. Encounters with behavioural problems are such intense experiences for all involved, and the context (be it classroom, off-site unit or manager's office) from which such behaviour is viewed no doubt influences these perspectives. Nevertheless, it is hoped that the findings presented in this discussion paper encourage open debate and that the key questions raised in the text provide some focus for useful interchange and reflection. To further this aim, the conclusion summarises and extends the issues involved in each of these categories.

Exclusion as removal suggested a viewpoint which, however reluctantly, gave primacy to the rights of the majority in a school community. Its purpose was to protect, by reducing offending behaviours within the school through removing and therefore essentially 'incapacitating' the offender. A feeling of rejection and of failing the excluded child could accompany this action and was certainly experienced as such by many of the excluded pupils interviewed and the educational professionals involved with them. One underlying concern was that, in protecting the majority, exclusion as removal involved some abnegation of responsibility for an individual who, in exhibiting behavioural difficulties, might actually be expressing needs. Key questions covered how far schools could reflect on their own understanding of and contribution to offending behaviours and whether there was, in the current context, sufficient support and acclaim for schools' efforts to retain and remedy problematic behaviours. Beyond that, it may be worth considering how far schools, with their current curriculum imperatives are actually able to take responsibility for – and resource – pupils' social and personal development. Should the right to remove socially dysfunctional pupils be better matched by a clear statutory requirement to teach the skills and thinking underpinning responsible behaviour? Indeed, is some kind of a National Curriculum for personal, social and moral growth now a particular need?

Exclusion as reprisal reflected a viewpoint which saw the need for some 'symbolic denunciation' of inappropriate behaviour. Its purpose was, in part, retributive: redress for the perceived victim, a deserved consequence - or 'price to pay' - which operated as a general deterrent and also resulted in such contrition that the offender was induced not to repeat their action. Yet, the pupil data provided here suggested that, in many instances, exclusion was neither a deterrent nor a pathway to remorse, reform and reintegration. Exclusion as reprisal was resisted in many instances, and it was parental corroboration which often seemed a key factor in acceptance of the sanction. Hence, it may be useful to consider other sanction strategies by re-examining what are the elements and processes of reprisals which do achieve reform. Here, the work of criminology theorists such as Ashworth (1983) and Braithwaite (1989) may be a relevant reference. 'Shame' at disappointing those to whom we are emotionally bonded, punitive confrontation which nevertheless distinguishes between offence and offender, support for a change of self-image in relation to previous behaviour, and forgiveness are the constituents which they identify, and the process is called 'reintegrative shaming'. Could schools and communities devise sanction scenarios which seek to incorporate these ingredients? One such deliberate example from Australian schools is Community Accountability Conferencing (CACs) where victims, offenders and those closely connected to them or the incident talk out its impact with trained mediators, with agreed action and outcomes.

Exclusion as remedy conveyed a viewpoint which suggested that mainstream education was not the most appropriate setting for meeting the particular needs of some children at least at certain times in their development. Exclusion thus provided a means of accessing the right sort of specialised support for those needs. Questions here covered how far exclusion as remedy currently allowed opportunities for recovery and reintegration and whether a remedy could or should be delivered via the punitive rejection of a person. Testimonies of the desire for rehabilitation after an exclusion were evident in the pupil sample, suggesting again that it might be useful to look in depth at the components of those recovery stories, with a view to considering how far they could be replicated cost-effectively in mainstream education. Small group settings, therapeutic intervention, alternative learning experiences, positive and sustained relationships with key adults who offer respect and regard, training pupils in managing emotions and behaviour seemed some of the recurring features, as well as accepting any progress would be slow and painstaking. Support for staff who deal with behaviour difficulties may also be a key issue. All this again suggests there is a need for schools and practitioners to be skilled in actually **understanding** behaviour and not just **managing** it.

Finally, schools, LEAs and above all government might all have to question whether the provision of strategies, resources and training for addressing behavioural difficulties has been a major omission in their educational policy and practice in the recent past.

REFERENCES

ASHWORTH, A. (1983) *Sentencing and Penal Policy.* London: Weidenfeld and Nicholson Ltd.

BERRIDGE, D. and BRODIE, I. (forthcoming) 'Residential child care in England and Wales: the enquiries and after'. In: Hill, M. and Aldgate, J. (eds) *Child Care in the United Kingdom and Ireland.* London: Jessica Kingsley.

BRAITHWAITE, J. (1989) *Crime, shame and reintegration.* Cambridge: Cambridge University Press.

BRODIE, I. (1995) *Highlight: Exclusion From School.* London: National Children's Bureau.

GREAT BRITAIN. DEPARTMENT FOR EDUCATION (1994) *Code of Practice on the identification and assessment of special educational needs.* London: DfE.

GILLBORN, D. (1995) 'Racism and exclusions from school: case studies in the denial of educational opportunity', paper presented at the European Conference on Educational Research (ECER 95). University of Bath, September.

HAYDEN, C. (1994) 'Primary age children excluded from school: a multi agency focus for concern', *Children and Society.* **8**; 3 pp 257-273.

HAYDEN, C. (1995) 'Primary school children excluded from school: numbers, characteristics, reasons and circumstances', paper presented at the European Conference on Educational Research (ECER 95). University of Bath, September.

O'CONNELL, T. and THORSBORNE, M. (1995) 'Conferencing: A restorative approach to interventions for serious incidents of harm in the school setting'. In: Conway, R. and IZARD, J. (eds). *Behaviour Outcomes: Choosing Appropriate Paths.* ACER (Australian Council for Educational Research).

OFFICE FOR STANDARDS IN EDUCATION (1996) *Exclusions from Secondary School 1995-96.* London: OFSTED

PARSONS, C. (1996) 'Permanent Exclusions from Schools in England in the 1990s: Trends, Causes and Responses'. *Children and Society* **10**; 3.

APPENDIX

PERCEPTIONS OF EXCLUSION:
a summary

Exclusion as ...	... removal	... reprisal	... remedy
believes:	• protection for majority must come first • need for 'incapacitation' of offender • schools cannot handle/resource these problems	• there is a 'price to pay' for misbehaviour • the need for a deterrent to others • sanctions create contrition and reform	• more suitable provision can be accessed • in the best interest of the child
can result in:	• relief for school community • sense of rejection by pupil • sense of failing the child	• acceptance of the reprisal (fast or slow track) • resistance to the reprisal (antagonism/ indifference) • little sense of deterrent to others	• access to specialised support • need for opportunities for re-integration
may require [instead]:	• an examination of school-factors affecting behaviour problems • acknowledgement/ criteria to value schools who do retain children with behavioural difficulties • a 'National Curriculum' for teaching personal/ social/moral education	• parental involvement and support • new sanction scenarios which create reform: - distinguishing between offence and offender - positive sustained relations with individual adults - support for behaviour change - focused learning environment	• training in the understanding as well as management of behaviour • replication of remediating factors in mainstream schools:

PUPIL RESPONSES TO EXCLUSION

	ACCEPTANCE of exclusion	RESISTANCE of exclusion
IMMEDIATE RESPONSE Exclusion is experienced as ...	distress/ emotional discomfort	escape/fun
LONGER-TERM OUTCOME Exclusion results in ...	contrition/regret	antagonism/ indifference

In rank order:

RESISTANCE	ACCEPTANCE
• extrication: feeling of escape/relief/ fun	
	• resolve to improve behaviour
	• feeling of distress/emotional discomfort
	• sanction severity reinforced by parents
	• displeasure at missing school (social)
• feeling of injustice/antagonism to school	
• nil-impact/no change	
• indifference	
• kudos	
• adverse effect on work	• concern about parental reaction
• problem of reintegration	
	• impact on return/academic consequences
	• advantageous to other pupils